All That She Ever Felt

Aaditi Bhambhani

ISBN: 978-93-340-0856-2

This book is dedicated to every soul that knows sky's the limit and are aware of the fact that sky is just a concept.
It is for all those who feel and believe that being alive means to feel each and every emotion till its peak.

Preface

Hello, dear reader.

The book contains the words and emotions that you are already familiar with but we often forget about them. In the hustle of life we forget to feel. These were the words I yearned to hear from someone else, yet they ultimately echoed within me.
I wish you can feel every emotion till it's depth as I believe we need to feel every moment and every emotion and feeling is what tells us that we are alive.

Thank you for choosing this book to read. I hope you find something that inspires you, resonates with you, fills you with hope and joy and challenges you to live your life how you want it. Because in the end it's your life and only you can decide how you wanna live it. We are made of the choices that we make.

Untouched by your version of me

All That She Ever Felt

Obsessed with the rain, that's me
Engrossed in the novel, that's me
Dancing with headphones, that's me
Forgetting random stuff, that's me
The imperfections that you see, that's me
It's beautiful, yeah, because it's me

Dear me
Is it necessary to be this dramatic
Or be every time sarcastic
Is it necessary to beat the shit
Or tell people they aren't your fit
Is it necessary to get into trouble
Or to pop fears like they are bubble
Is It necessary to do something and then think
Or taking everything as you can do it in blink
Is it necessary to drive like you have two lives
Or walk with a tongue sharp as knives
I know it's not easy to consume all the hurt
silently
But see you handle all of it so patiently
Dear me you know I love you
Just don't call your brain for rescue
You have a very very beautiful heart
And be sure to stay same for every end and start

What are the parts of you that are unheard but
true
you lived through them but nobody has any clue
What are the words that never came out
The thoughts that lived through your doubts
What's the part of your life you never shared
The moments when you were the only one who
cared
When was the time you gulped your anger with a
sigh
The times when you wanted to forget pain by
getting high
But somewhere in between the high and the low
You made sure what you had you didn't throw
And there wasn't just shadows that were hidden
in the dark
All the smiles you hid so that one day you can be
fire from just the spark

All That She Ever Felt

She wasn't someone who can stay in a cage
The world could easily burn in her rage
Her mind was a roller coaster for thoughts
And she was a mastermind in planning plots
She would smile and hear you lie
Because she knew the truth you would never defy
Some Days she was stuck on hard and dark days
But she alone fought them and found her ways
One could never survive her aura and energy
As she was a beauty until you force her to use strategy
She had the wings which were chopped many times
Little did they know they were committing crimes
No she wasn't gonna stop and follow what she was told
She made her own decisions as she was fearless and bold
No cost can ever match her freedom of open sky
Try to walk over her peace of mind and be ready to die

All That She Ever Felt

Did someone ask for your opinion
Or you think only you are capable to make a
decision
What made you think you had a point
Are yours and my life joint
How could you think that I'll face the same
When your mind is stable and mine is insane
I heard you talking behind my back
Saying she's mad and doesn't have a track
Let me tell you I would never waste my words on
you
I hold the amount of power that could tighten all
your screw
Oh wait but your talk never reached my brain
Maybe it got washed away in drain
Just so as to give you a heads up
I'll tolerate you till you overflow my cup
After that you won't speak in front of me again
Because I would prove you that your life is vain

All That She Ever Felt

I want a life not a cage
To be not on the ground but stage
I want to live like a free breeze
To make most of moments as they freeze
I want to smile after shedding tears
To watch ashes of all my fears
I want the mirror to reflect who I am
To watch people look at me like, damn!
I don't want to be accessible to everyone
But to choose if they deserve All of me or none
I don't want to chase what turned me Grey
But to change myself like I was clay
I don't want to stop myself from crashing down
But to unmask every person hiding like clown
I wanna run towards the inevitable
And make each of them my favorite fairytale

All That She Ever Felt

She lived in her own world
Taking paths which were twirled
Her eyes only reflected sparkled dreams
Each day filled with unfigured themes
One would never hear stress in her voice
Cause the decisions she took were her choice
She paused when it became too much
Ignored those eyes which existed only to judge
Her priority was to live life as it comes
To celebrate smallest achievement with drums
She embraced all the emotions she ever felt
Had a heart that would make anyone melt
Her presence turned the room bright from dull
Leaving everyone hard to mumble
No she never escaped reality
But her perspective saw things differently

They left me broken on the ground
I turned back, they were not around
I wished that I couldn't trust again
But there was a voice in my brain
They did you bad doesn't mean it's you
You can't change if you were true
You can't stop feeling the love
You can't change when you are pure as dove
It's okay, what they did is their loss
If they couldn't accept you with your flaws
You can't change what someone does
But changing yourself for that is curse
It takes a lot to be gentle and kind
Even when life gives you pain in rewind
Don't ever regret what you felt and gave
Because you are suppose to carry happiness, not
pain to your grave

Why do you look like you don't care
How do you always carry magic in your stare
How do you hear everything and still smile
How can you walk by yourself from mile to mile
Why do you not think about what left
Why do you not convince about what you suggest
How can you be so furious yet so calm
Even in the toughest time how do you still have charm
Does the glass you walk on doesn't hurt you
I am at peace with myself is actually true
I started to step ahead for me and not you
I cry about few reasons but only once not two
If you ask me am I not scared to keep myself first
I took that glass of water after desert full of thirst
So I'll do it over and over again
Because I'm not someone you can get in bargain

All That She Ever Felt

Oh you lied a times few
Now I'm staring right back at you
you thought you could get away with it
Before that I'll just repay you every bit
Although feel glad for chances you got
But now it's time for you to rot
I'm not gonna wait for it to happen
When all it could do is threaten
Weren't you the one blaming me
Now you have the subscription of my game free
Yeah I'll enjoy watching you lose
Because that's what you choose
I spared you once, twice, thrice
Now I'm the cat and you are my mice

They say don't buy rose they die
If you are strong you won't cry
Don't feel momentarily joy
It will do nothing but destroy
I don't know what to reply
But their conditions I can't apply
Even if weird, they make me happy
I like it even if it is crappy
I'll rather do it than regret
Experience what I will never forget
Maybe they are right and I am wrong
But my life isn't their song
I'll buy the rose if it makes me smile
I'll keep it, even if it gets out of style
I know what means the world for me
And no it doesn't bother me how they see

To be strong is not to hide feelings
To be strong is not to hide your dealings
To be strong is not avoid looking down
To be strong is not to change subject with a frown
To be strong is not to stop visiting those places
To be strong is not to join again those races
To be strong is not letting it go to forget everything
To be strong is not pulling every string
To be strong is to fall and feel it all
To be strong is to get up and stand tall
To be strong is letting yourself try all if you believe
To be strong is to never being afraid of the leap
To be strong is to love yourself at worse
To be strong is to know you trying is not curse
To be strong is to stand up and be real
To be strong is to let yourself be hurt and heal
To be strong is to setting them free without leaving
To be strong is to still move on but be there when
they need saving
To be strong is to go through everything you feel in
To be strong is to feel that you are complete from
within

All That She Ever Felt

Get up and Buy yourself roses
Compile yourself in unlimited proses
You are not meant to be in a cage
You are as holy as a sage
It's a pity when you let go of your dream
When you hide your emotions without a scream
Stand in front of the mirror and stare
All your Thorns and petals are for you to care
How can you turn your eyes and not see
That you are capable of everything you wanna be
Your eyes hold the beauty and your shine
Every inch of you begging you to say you are
mine
Stop giving yourself what ifs and buts
Because you are still smiling despite thousand
cuts
Stop listening to those who says you are too free
Because you are like air, breeze or thunder who
you choose to be
Your life should revolve around your heart
It's should be your choices and desires that set
you apart

All That She Ever Felt

I can easily become a bitch
But there is always this glitch
I'm also sweet and really kind
But I want to go out of my mind
I bled all over their knives
Even when I had the power to destroy their lives
I want to be ruthless and so cruel
But I can't jump from that patient stool
I love my pure light side of feminine
But how to make myself understand being dark is only adrenaline
It's fine if you give them what they deserve
But knowing it was I they couldn't preserve
I wouldn't mind giving them their taste
But why should I let my energy go in waste
I did everything for their best
And they couldn't understand I was better than rest
I'll let them have whatever they can take
Until the moment my mind says it's a break
that time they will regret it with all their power
Because it wasn't only mercy I could shower

Everybody thinks she is beautiful
And how can someone see everything so colorful
Little did they know every single night
She struggles to find something bright
Her heart craves for the kindness she provides
Wishes that everyone would be happy with what she decides
Everyday she hears one thing or the other
Pretending to everyone that she doesn't bother
Little did they know how her heart handles it
How everything just breaks her down bit by bit
Her eyes sparkle due to the presence of salty water
And her body asking her to get tougher
Even after that she doesn't fail to put a smile on her face
Believing that it will all be okay and this is just a phase

All That She Ever Felt

you know people will come and go but you will
stay
They will come and tell you to follow a way
They will make you question everything you do
Give your heart scars and turn it blue
They will do whatever it takes to make you
insecure
There words are like poison without cure
But you can't fall into that trap
Because you are not the one who is crap
Your heart and mind are someone's special place
Some love you as they know you are someone
they can't replace
My love you will have all kinds of people around
you
Don't care about all just focus on few
you are you and the best person I ever knew
You shine whether you are alone or in a crew

They say abide by the rules
Wear them like they are jewels
I hear it's not in your limits
Bear the pain its just bullets
If you step out you will lose that reputation
I see its something out of your expectation
But dear each time you cut those wings
And hope that I follow same rings
Take a guess i won't let you win
Stop your words before they even begin
For now all you see is my stare
And it's too much for you to bear
Try it, test my patience
And I promise I will burn you in my radiance

Hey I heard what you said behind my back
But it didn't even make a crack
Oh watching me now it's hurting you
I hope what you are saying is true
Am I being too rude
You think it's gonna bother me dude
You tried to bring me down again and again
And I'm watching your hard work going in vain
Cause yeah for once raise your head see
Whose life are you still hooked on it's me
Tchtch see where it lead you and where it lead me
You are still a Brooke but babe I'm the whole sea

All That She Ever Felt

People will come and go
Cause they are a river with constant flow
But despite all the difficulties you grow
Turn those scars into something that make you
glow
Even in the darkest of nights
You showed yourself to the field of lights
Even in the silenced screams
You made sure you carried your dreams
Sometimes your hopes kept you alive
You stayed with yourself while you revive
You are your biggest support and should be
Because nobody else can make you realize what
you could do when you are free

She seems kind but she's fierce
It will only take her a moment to bring you to tears
You cannot control her internal flame
If you try to then you and your ashes will look same
You can sure try to put her off with water
But hey look just something to remember
It may take a little time but she's going to reignite
And that my friend will be your last night
So you gotta stay out of her way
Try but she won't listen to you anyway
It took her a lot to make her who she is
But still she is not the one you try to piss

All That She Ever Felt

There are days that you don't want to leave the
bed
When you just wish you were dead
When your eyes do not go dry
It's so hard to even give it one more try
It feels that no life is left within you
Neither you want anyone to come for rescue
You have been numb for so many moments
That feeling anything again is like winning a
tournament
When you don't wanna justify what you do
And that you is not anymore you
But there is something beating within
That actually wish that you will win
It confirms that it's not going to be dark forever
But till then you gotta keep it all together
No one can actually change it for you
So it's time that you get up and do

No I don't have my shit together
But still I don't want you to bother
No I don't care about your solutions
Even if all options are not clear but confusions
No I can't hear you speaking your words
And yes I know when you say you feel unheard
Still you think I don't listen cause I have attitude
Don't you ever think for you it's my aptitude
No I am not busy to not find time
But you are not a part of life that's mine
Maybe your intentions are not bad
But can't you see it's not you I'm mad
No it's not your part to decide
To set the boundaries I'm supposed to abide
remember I can't walk on the path you choose
Even if that make you think my screws are loose
Because just like you I have one life too
So I'll do everything like I want even if it turns me
blue

Who knew what she was hiding
Who knew what was that she was fighting
Who knew why she was smiling
Who knew why she was always trying
Who knew why her words had warmth
Who knew why she was sometimes in wrath
Who knew what was behind her word
Who knew why she was always a nerd
Who knew how many thoughts raced in her mind
Who knew why she was always kind
Nobody knew her how she knew herself
She didn't need anyone cause she was her elf

All That She Ever Felt

Some scars are meant to stay hidden
Some promises are meant to be broken
Some mistakes can never be forgiven
Some people are undertaken
Some actions are mistaken
Sometimes tears are to be fallen
Some words can never be outspoken
Situations cannot worsen
The road ahead can not be darken
When Happiness has been stolen
It's not planned but all of a sudden
There is no strength but you are weaken
And every decision was wrong, its proven
And all you gotta do is stay unshaken
Because only you can turn yellow to golden

There are way too many lies
No one can ever find them all even if they tries
They manipulate it with words
Thinking there is no reason it's absurd
They would cry in front but can still be laughing
behind
Feeling happy how they fucked your mind
But yes you got used again
So might as well hide your tears in rain
You know you put yourself in that position
Your heart took away your mind's function
See your face still holds a smile
Yeah it hides the pain of being broken for more
than a while
Maybe it's like a knife that leaves you bleeding
within
But that strength will let you fall into rhythm
It's them they will be what they choose
But it's on you if wanna win or lose

All That She Ever Felt

I'm tired of hurting myself because of their deeds
I'm tired of defending them even when they were
weeds
i'm tired of being someone who always
understands
I'm tired of being stuck in the cycle that never
ends
I'm tired of validating others feelings before mine
I'm tired of being the bigger person every time
I'm tired of listening and feeling
I'm tired of explaining myself that they need
healing
I'm tired of being kind in the world that is toxic
and selfish
I'm tired of being called devilish
I'm tired of treating everyone as if they are my
heart
I'm tired of being the one that is torn apart

When I was all warm and nice
But you gave me in return, hard ice
I stayed calm and accepted the fight
Cause, baby, in my dictionary it wasn't right
It isn't the end as you are thinking
My eyes are watching you without blinking
I haven't forgotten how I cried
My silence will let you keep your pride
I'll suggest that from now on you watch your
steps
Cause I was just preoccupied with preps
And even though I feel karma is real
I would love to apply the seal
Behind all that cute and innocent face
My mind was the thing you couldn't trace
It's because my heart takes the decisions
And if Hurt they switch positions
All my fury and rage is looking out for you
And if you couldn't believe your fault cause it's
true

Yeah she got the nerve
Grabbing everything she deserve
All her thoughts pointing to indecisiveness
Meanwhile treating herself like the highness
Jumping on the bed thinking it's cloud
Your words unheard cause music's too loud
Call her out and she will be there to save
Being the company you crave
Her dreams can make you scream
Innocent yet can perfectly scheme
Sometimes she spends her night gazing at stars
Not a superwoman but got all powers
She's glittery and can feel like magic
Cause she is the unforgettable classic

It's okay to fail
To feel that you are off the trail
When nothing feels right
Just hug yourself closely and tight
For now Even if it's night
The sun is waiting to rise and shine bright
You know you carry it around
The sparkle of the diamond trying best to be
found
It may take some time
But you can make lemonade with the lime
Just have that faith in you
There is no one and never will be like you
It depends on you how you want it to be
To accept you can't grow and stay a seed or fight
to be a tree

All That She Ever Felt

Even if it takes thousand of days
Redoing it in different ways
Even if it feels like you won't reach there
Ask yourself should you even care
When you know it's you
Then today or tomorrow it will be true
People will say thousand words
But they shouldn't be the one you heard
Listen to what your heart has to say to you
The sky is grey now but it will be blue
If you cross all the walls that are made
Once you reach there all your pain will fade
Without a word and another doubt
Trust your gut , make yourself proud
Allow your dream to consume all you got
Even if you fail you know at least you fought

Why would I laugh when I don't want to
Why would I even smile just to please you
Am I not allowed to be as my emotions say
Why I always have to follow a way
Can't I just ignore it and move silently
Why I have to speak pleasantly
Why I can't be my own sunshine
After the day which burnt me and didn't leave a
line
Why there is a question mark after i let my
thoughts tell me
Why I cant let my opinions fell with glee
What's my life will you tell me
I'm not sorry for not letting you select for me

I am the strength
they couldn't break
I wasn't the one fake,
that's what they couldn't take

All That She Ever Felt

Was the sky really so blue
Or was it something I never knew
It wasn't my mind that was confused
But I stepped into it without being pursued
Was i supposed to hold it or let it go
I was wandering in it without flow
Like i just walked into an other side
Where there were No rules which I had to abide
It wasn't just a moment but a feeling
There wasn't effort but scars were healing
There was no second where I had to pretend
I didn't knew if it was sticking to me till the end
I wasn't scared but all ready to find it out
And explore every inch of what I found

All That She Ever Felt

Some saw love as burning red
In the books of proses dried and dead
Some experienced love as potion to their scars
In the deep and dark night as glistening stars
Some say love appeared and vanished in blink of
an eye
Because instead of fighting hard they let it go with
a sigh
Some found love in forgiveness as second chance
In the memory of those who stole heart at first
glance
Some feel love ages like fine wine
Picks you up from the ground and drops on cloud
nine
Some seek love in the form of attraction and care
After getting broken time and again one last dare
But what if love is beyond all the conceptions and
misconceptions
What if at a single time you only feel a fraction
What if love can never end up in a line or sentence
Because it steps into the hearts without entrance
It stays there in the form of smile or pain
And states that devoid of the person love always
remain

you call yourself ordinary
But how can I explain to you that you are my
imaginary
you tell me that I deserve someone better
When in front of you nobody else even matter
you tell me that you haven't achieved anything
great
And that being with you is my mistake
How can I tell you that you are my safest place
And that I wanna escape with you where no one
can ever trace
you are sometimes unsure about how you look
But baby it's your soul that kept me hooked
No words, no music, no poetry can ever justify
what I feel for you
Because you turned golden what was once blue
But in every silence that has to be loud
you are my peaceful cloud
And no you don't have to be insecure about
anyone else
Because my love you matter to me more than
what I'm for myself

Sometimes I allow my thoughts to go wild
Where everything is tempting and not mild
My lips asking for just one more kiss
Just to embrace the perfect moment of bliss
Your hand caressing my tender face
Other wandering on me leaving trace
My breaths all deep and slow
And that love is all that we know
I cannot explain how it felt when you felt me
My fingers tangled in yours still felt free
Your eyes providing me with all the shine
while You whispered you are all mine
Everything was so bright and new
My body following your rhythm as it knew
I know I'll never forget what you gave me
The moment when you and I became we

I know you might
Be looking into that night
When I was lying in your arms
And it wasn't just our charms
I wasn't drunk and neither were you
But all we felt was just so new
It was expected from time to slow down
There was no rush to run back to town
My eyes reflected yours back
Heartbeats hard to track
It wasn't shiny or made with gold
Everything was understood without being told
It was just one word to a long book
Which could be forgotten without another look
That time was stolen from fantasy
What was to come is just mystery
But in that moment i knew
It was too real to be considered true

I want to know why you always push me
For the things that matter but others can't see
I want to know why you support my decisions
When others can't see future for my suggestions
I want to know why you ask me like you are
entitled to
When you never said anything when I wanted to
be with you
I want to know why are you putting so much
efforts now
And why I should let myself trust you, like how
Yes it's bothering me since the day you came
again
Making me remember that sunshine and rain
I can't let you make me feel what I anyways felt
Because my heart broke by seeing how you left
Yes you were mesmerizing and incredible to me
But I left you when you said you and I couldn't be
I don't have any space for you in my heart
you chose the distance and turned us from close
to apart

To pain, to past
To feelings that didn't last
May we never meet again
Because from you
there is nothing I could now gain

All That She Ever Felt

I wish I could hold you in my arms
Give you each of my lucky charms
I wish I could make your problems disappear
Solve each one of them so you could be happier
I wish I could admire you when you sleep
Give you long hugs and cuddles when you wanna
weep
I wish I could take care of you when you forget to
And make you feel that there's no one like you
I wish I could give you all I had
Calm you down when something makes you mad
I wish I could be there to make your life easy
But I try to provide my warmth even if it's freezy
I wish I could provide you the comfort of my
presence
But I know we are parted by distance
I wish we achieve what we want soon
And you could have me during each phase of
moon

So many stars lie in the galaxy
But he was the one from her fantasy
She was a beauty filled with imperfections
But from all of it there was just one perfection
He wouldn't bend until it's for her
Even at the moment of anger it stayed fur
Sometimes demons of insecurity, misjudgement
took over
But fighting it together brought them more closer
They settled within each other like jigsaw puzzle
The love they have was not like storm but drizzle
Every time I think what love is
Theirs is the best story that leave me in bliss
Their eyes prove that they flow in each other's
veins
And may what they have always remain

All That She Ever Felt

I own the right to kiss you and call you mine
I own the right to call you any time
I own the right to jump and hug you
I own the right to put you under my curfew
I own the right to every one of your clothes
I own the right to turn true every one of your hopes
I own the right to play with your dimples and cheeks
I own the right to make you feel every emotion till your peak
I own the right to touch you whenever I want to
I own the right to tell you what you can or cannot do
I own the right to tell everyone who you belong with
I own the right to turn every moment into beautiful fact from myth
And no one can ever take that right away from me
If they even try , their scariest dream is what I'll be
No I can't stand the possibility of anyone trying to get you
Because you are not common but unique, beautiful and my dream come true

All That She Ever Felt

We saw each other grow
Been there from dull to full glow
What started with huge silence
And of course with a little violence
Has now turned into something incredible
Where separation is unbearable
Sometimes the words may lie
But looking in eyes we can't deny or defy
What this is or how it's gonna be
But you will always be my happy eve
you may shout or doubt
But when it's me you will know it all about
Distance can tear us apart
But like it's said we own each other's biggest part

you randomly came into my way
And despite my tries decided to stay
I wanted to kick you out
But now you know all my whereabouts
I was confused with the changes you brought
But followed it all without any thought
I asked what are you trying to do
you replied bringing that love song to you
I was scared that I'll blew everything
You hold me and said it's just the beginning
I couldn't believe that all of it was true
You peeked into my eyes and provided the clue
You became my sun and I sparkled in your light
And my happily ever after became to hold you
tight

All That She Ever Felt

You make my days brighter
And turn the chilly cold nights warmer
I smile everytime I think of you
It's like I met someone I always knew
I fall short of words everytime I try to describe
It's like you are not a human but my favorite vibe
Sometimes I cry looking at those tiny effort
Even on those hard times you provide me comfort
I can never tell you how much you mean to me
But I can promise I'll always be there, guarantee

All That She Ever Felt

All That She Ever Felt

I wanna talk to you about your day
I wanna follow you on your way
I wanna keep my hand on your waist
I wanna make you feel embraced
I wanna notice the glow in your eyes
I wanna see you enjoy your fries
I wanna watch you when you're on fire
I wanna watch you filled with desire
I wanna see you fall and shine again
Every little detail I wanna maintain
Never saw never knew anybody like you
You say you flawed but I don't feel it's true
I want you and your presence to stay
But you are far far awayyy

All That She Ever Felt

I might smile but don't feel
I might cry but won't heal
I might speak but without words
It's the noise but still unheard
I shiver when I try to stand
Every direction look like a dead end
You came and then you left
Stole my heart but I couldn't call it theft
I wasn't wrong and you weren't too
When it happened you too felt it true
Your words are echoing in my brain
I lost more than what I had to gain
My heart wasn't strong for what happened
Why did you leave my hand when destiny
threatened
I'm afraid I won't fall in love again with another
As it broke me when you said we could be friends
but not together

No I don't hate love after what happened
It wasn't less or more than what I imagined
Honestly loving unconditionally is the best thing
It's like two individuals tied with a string
To love is to provide all of who you are
To have something that is sweet and sour
But when you give roses you have thorns too
Like standing on a cliff watching mesmerizing view
What I'm scared of is being the only one to jump
Being the only one to fight against every bump
even after I chose that person above my self
respect
They chose to leave and all I could do was accept
No I can't put myself through same tears and pain
My body trembling with shivers and my mind totally
drain
Where food is left untouched and I'm losing weight
When all I see is blurry surface all day lying in bed
straight
I don't care if now I become ruthless and burn the
world down
But I'm no longer willing to wear the I'm in love
crown

All That She Ever Felt

I find it hard to describe it to you
It feels like somewhere the words flew
I can't ever tell you how much you mean to me
Cause words in my brain set letters free
None of my sentences make sense
So I guess magic is it's essence
The fragrance of what you and I share
It can never be captivated cause it's rare

All That She Ever Felt

I knew where it will lead
you and me together wasn't a good deed
you were looking for a secret escape
When I walked in wearing a black drape
Making it hard for you to breathe
I stared at you and made way to leave
I knew you would take the chance
And not give it up proved your glance
What started slow couldn't end like that
We collided like we were tit for tat
I knew it wasn't going to last forever
In the morning we would disappear to meet never
But I bet you will always remember me while
going wild
Because even when we kissed it wasn't mild

you knew it, you knew it all
So why you turned indifferent on call
you knew I wasn't sweet and easy to keep
Didn't mean you left me alone to weep
I showed you all of my flaws
You listed them like some organizations clause
Every time I tried to leave
You held my hand and started to grieve
I never told you I was turning cold
You treated me like ash after saying I was gold
I watched you turn me from innocent to cruel
After you made me break all of the rule
I remember how you went all to nothing
I still love you but my heart isn't breathing
Tell me how to rewind and leave you on read
Because now I think I could be better if I didn't
cared

All That She Ever Felt

When you fall
I'm here always who you can call
When you feel you are not okay
I'm here to make or save the day
When you don't wanna talk
Then we can go for a walk
If you feel distance is too much
And you miss me and my touch
Hold on to the thought that you are mine
And I'll be next to you when it's time
When I throw tantrums upon you
It's just because I want your attention too
When you don't wanna do anything
I assure you still you will be able to achieve
everything
Why you have to fear
When I'm here
Baby you are mine And I'm sorry if I bother you
And I know you love me too

I'm not happy but I'm not sad either
He doesn't want it back and me neither
my thoughts are loud but his are silent
My hurt was quiet his was violent
All I did was stay and try to resolve
but with me he wasn't ready to evolve
He left when I kept holding it on
before I tried to stop he was already gone
I get it You were broken I was too
but when I was ready to fix, why weren't you
It was not always a deserted night
it once was shiny and sparkly bright
where there was love in our presence
how can now we find peace in each others
absence
he was moving in chain I wanted to break it
My fault was that I thought he wanted to make it
but it fired back against me and I lost it all
I still believe it can be solved with just a call
He gave up, stood silent and went all dry
when all I still wanted was to try

I get it I get it all
They always expect you to stand tall
Even if you got a thousand cuts
Smile without any ifs or buts
When the pain becomes unbearable
Don't you run away, it's terrible
You can't return it to the giver
Hold it the anxiety it give with shiver
I wanna face those who did it
Ask how did they decide I wasn't great fit
After I gave away everything I had
They left by saying I was the one bad
I wanna shout from rage and fire
No rules can stop me from getting what I desire
Even if the scars break me again and again
I dare them to stop me from becoming what they
can't bargain

All That She Ever Felt

Yes I was wrong but so were you
I felt it to be true and you did too
Why did you let it all slip away
Why couldn't you make me Stay
Why did you have to lie on my face
How could you think I won't be able to trace
How could you change just like that
Say things that added deep crack
I pleaded you to stop changing me
But you couldn't stop to make me change even my
dream
You broke me and now I'm lying in pieces
I never knew what was whole eventually
decreases
I love you and I can't stop or hate you
Because once I thought you were better than
those few

All That She Ever Felt

I wanna see you smile
Hold you in every while
Take away all the sad history
Let every moment be a mystery
I know sometimes it gets tough
When we feel like it's just not enough
But what if we just hold on
Lie sleepy with each other and just yawn
No I'll never find another like you
Why? Because you are the love which is true
I know I mess bad sometimes
But other days I'm your ray which always shines
I promise to be forever yours
Because we have something that is completely
ours

How can you say that magic is not true
Have you seen the place I grew
Where each rain brings rainbow
Where moon creates my shadow
Where the night sky is filled with stars
Where the air heal the scars
Where I learnt everything from nature
Where peace flows through every creature
I can see the clouds making shapes
Sun shining through them creating escapes
The magnificent scene of colors and hue
Birds floating in the sky blue
Where happiness will flow in your vein
Where each memory will be like a pretty stain
I know you won't believe me
Because for you this sight Is the dream you
wanna see

All That She Ever Felt

I turned 19 under the stars
Telling myself be proud of your scars
I looked up and said happy birthday
Your smile would always make you okay
Reminding that age is just a number
Turning old won't make you less of a blunder
You will have your highs and lows
But stay as you want from your head to toes
Some people will love and some will hate you
But only you know your version which is true
All have changed in a year but all is same
Everything went to become stable but I stayed insane
Now it's time that I bid the number a goodbye
And welcome another year with a warm hi
Raising a toast to never forgetting living a teenage dream
Doesn't matter if I'm with myself or in a team

All That She Ever Felt

you said that you would
But you lied when you could
I kept postponing the lines
you crossed them saying you are mine
I took you as a favorite song
Little did you know I can be thunderstorm
you saw the side that was sweet
But after I knew all you did was cheat
My love for you turned to despise
Now it's your turn to pay the prize
I smiled and told you goodbye
Guess you didn't realized you were about to die
No I wouldn't let you escape easily
I'll take my revenge fearlessly
Until I think it got us even
Stay calm darling, it's just beginning

Being soft and kind is my pride
There are no boundaries I abide
There is no pain in my eyes
My heart is still a child, just wise
Your words reach my ears but are unheard
My life is no longer black and white but colored
I feel every inch of emotion within me
Cause I no longer care how others see
If it makes me happy I'll do it
There is no mold I aspire to fit
I know sometimes it can pull me down
But I'll make it again cause I wear my crown
It's a privilege if I allow you in my life
But if you hurt I'll have a knife
There is more to me than what you'll ever know
Cause I can be hard ice or soft snow
My kindness and softness I'll maintain
Just don't be the one to drive me insane

All That She Ever Felt

Instead of thinking one thing over
Think till the sight can cover
Instead of sympathizing yourself
Grab every skill from the shelf
Instead of losing all the power
Add double fuel cause you got to empower
Believing you can't, oh no it's crime
Just remind yourself from time to time
All the sparks are ready to come out
You are not letting them light up in doubt
Everything will revolve around you
Once you know that you can make it come true

Life is like a work of art
Clean canvas it is at start
We add colors not only our own
From all the places not just our home
Every stroke of the timeline we have been in
Of all the losses and every win
Texture of every skin we ever felt
Tone of every feeling we ever dealt
Sometimes we tried to copy from our inspiration
And heard things that we forgot it was our creation
The goal of it is not to have it perfect
But let it be you and what all you expect
The canvas will be full one day and it will all end
You think you will be here for your choices to defend
Paint the light you want to feel
Or the darkness from which you wanna heal
Allow the canvas to be all you wanna be
To let your soul and mind always be free

ABOUT THE AUTHOR

Hey, I guess you all already know a lot of stuff about the author. Still I would like to introduce myself a bit. My name is Aaditi and I am so much more than what I will ever be able to convey. Art and efforts are my priorities. Music flows in my veins and my favorite touch is that of rain.

Always remember one thing: the pen is in your hand and the rest of the story is still unwritten. It's okay to fail but if you know it's you and if something is coming from your heart listen to it. The heart always knows. Maybe you don't know everything but if you know yourself and can feel you know enough.

In the end you can listen to Aye Zindagi (chalk N Duster) and Unwritten (Natasha Bedingfield)

Goodluck, be you always..

If you wanna leave feedback or connect:
aaditi.bhambhani@gmail.com